MW00860706

"This is a real and readat
panion during pain-fillec
mon feelings and experi ̶ ̶ ̶ ̶ ̶ ̶p̶ p̶e̶r̶-̶
sonal losses. Readable because the writing style flows easily and
smoothly. Practical because the commentaries contain insightful
observations and useful suggestions about suffering and healing.
Prayable because grief stricken individuals will find that the many
prayers in this volume capture their keenly felt sentiments."

Joseph M. Champlin
Author, *A Thoughtful Word, A Healing Touch*

"With compassion and empathy Evan Drake Howard addresses
those who are walking through the Valley of Shadows. These sen-
sitive prayers will touch men and women of various faith traditions. They help point us *through* the Valley toward meadows of
reassurance and healing."

Rabbi Leslie Yale Gutterman
Temple Beth-El, Providence, RI

"Powerless. Stuck. Going nowhere, and none too soon. This is the
grief walk, and faith often throws little relief (or hope!) our way.
Through brief, insightful, inviting little chapters and with very
honest, heart enlivening prayers, Evan Drake Howard offers a rich
treasure to those 'on the walk.'"

Rev. Richard B. Gilbert
Author, *HeartPeace: Healing Words for Hurting Folks*

"Funeral directors have long lamented the absence of a collection
of prayers that focus on the needs of the bereaved. *Suffering Loss,
Seeking Healing* is a valuable religious resource to share with those
seeking healing from the pain of loss."

Roger E. Osborne
Past President, Samaritans USA

"The wisdom of this book brings new beginnings and hope
through the courageous healing process of honest introspection,
prayer, and the friendship of God."

Dr. Rollin Karnehm, Psychotherapist

"*Suffering Loss, Seeking Healing* is a refreshing and courageous walk through the valley of despair up to the mountain of new life, from the crisis of personal loss to the joyful experience of God's grace. It is a healing experience!"

The Very Rev. Richard O. Singleton, Dean
The Episcopal Cathedral of St. John, Providence, RI

"These prayer-poems are as realistically sad, joyful, angry, and hopeful as the many-emotioned struggle through grief itself. This book should prove helpful to people experiencing the very thoughts and emotions Evan Drake Howard has managed to put into words so well."

Charles Meyer
Author, *Surviving Death: A Practical Guide to Caring for the Dying and Bereaved*

"Dr. Howard offers companionship to those going through what C. G. Jung called the *nekyia*, the dark night of the soul. The honesty and integrity of Dr. Howard's voice will offer comfort to fellow travelers who struggle along the way."

Linda Carter, R.N., M.S.N., C.S.
Diploma candidate, C.G. Jung Institute

"The journey through losses is a long and lonely one. The greatest support and understanding comes from the individual's God-connection. Evan Howard's prayers can help the grieving person express the depth of pain while embracing God's presence. It is *this* presence that leads to healing."

Dorothy Levesque
Ministry with Divorce and all other Losses
Diocese of Providence

"The two sections of this book, 'Expressing the Hurt' and 'Seeking the Healing,' follow a natural progression if, as Howard advises, the pray-er surrenders to the feelings that accompany great loss of any kind. The reader can browse through the chapters to choose those that fit the moment. Their universality is a tribute to the sensitivity of the writer."

Margot Hover, D.Min.
Author, *Caring for Yourself When Caring for Others*

Suffering Loss, Seeking Healing

Prayers for Pain-Filled Times

Evan Drake Howard

TWENTY-THIRD PUBLICATIONS

Mystic, CT 06355

Third printing 2001

Twenty-Third Publications
A Division of Bayard
185 Willow Street
P.O. Box 180
Mystic, CT 06355
(860) 536-2611
(800)321-0411
www.twentythirdpublications.com

ISBN 0-89622-699-9
Printed in the U.S.A.

Contents

Seeking the Healing

Dedication

In Memory of Ed, Julie, and Skipper

Introduction

You've lost someone or something dear to you, as dear as life itself, and you're devastated. Never have you experienced such trauma. Questions throb in your mind: Why did this happen? What will I do now? How can I ever recover? Your loss has changed your life, and there's no going back. How you respond will affect you for years to come.

If you've lost a loved one to death, you feel as though part of you has died, too. It's like an amputation, and you wonder how you can go on—or if you even want to. Call it unjust, unfair, unbearable. It's all of that, and worse. The words don't matter. All that matters is that death has robbed you of someone irreplaceable, and your heart has erupted in pain.

A divorce or the end of some other special relationship is also a death, and no less traumatic. This relationship gone, you feel empty and incomplete, haunted by a paralyzing loneliness, and you're tormented by the fear that you might be lonely forever.

Such losses initiate the grief process. So does being "downsized," fired, or laid off. So does failing to achieve an important educational or vocational goal. We grieve many times, in many different ways, throughout our lives. Whether having suffered physical disability or having moved to another part of the country, whether having no chance to become a parent or having to adjust to an empty nest, whether having failed morally or having been sexually abused as a child, whether having experienced financial ruin or having received a terminal diagnosis, we enter the grief process shaken to the core.

Suffering a major loss is life's deepest hurt, no matter what the loss may be. Grief evokes a powerful emotional response. The feelings associated with this response include, but are not limited to, shock, numbness, denial, anger, guilt, fear, and depression. Working through these feelings over time will, we hope, lead to acceptance, the ability to move on. We wish this process were easier, but it's not. In fact, coming to terms with grief is the hardest of all tasks.

I wrote these prayers to enter into the pain with you, one human being to another. They come from my heart to yours, expressing both the anguish of grief and the hope of faith. Like you, I have suffered significant losses, some tangible, others intangible. Numerous relocations have forced me to leave behind friends and beloved surroundings. I have been on the losing end of romantic relationships. Breaking my left leg deprived me of a degree of physical mobility. I have lost to death all my grandparents, my father, my father-in-law, and many friends. At midlife, I look back at dreams now shattered and youthful innocence now compromised by adult complexities. And then there have been my failures.

Where does one turn amid the agonizing grief of such losses? I have found solace in prayer. Prayer can't bring back what has been lost and it can't stop the pain; it can, though, give us a spiritual perspective on what has happened. These prayers can help you find this perspective. Although they rose out of my own experience, they echo the anguish that many grieving people have shared with me as a pastor.

One loss triggers memories of many others. This is why allowing yourself to grieve is a courageous discipline. Such discipline can foster understanding, emotional relief, and transformation. These qualities emerge when a spiritual perspective renders suffering meaningful, making it possible to integrate it into your life. This integration retrieves hope from the despair that inevitably accompanies meaningless suffering. This hope comes to those who respond to at least four challenges: the challenge of honesty, the challenge of resiliency, the challenge of receptivity, and the challenge of creativity.

If these prayers, organized to help you meet these challenges, accomplish their purpose, they will point the way toward a healthy grief process. They are for all who mourn. As a Christian pastor, my faith is grounded in God's love in Jesus Christ. But these prayers are based on the conviction that God suffers with everyone who grieves, regardless of religious affiliation. I hope that seekers from a diversity of backgrounds and traditions will find solace in these prayers during their time of need.

It will take time and grueling emotional work before you can rebuild your life and believe in a better future. But this will come as you persevere in the grief process for as long as it takes to get through it. These prayers are a resource for your journey. May they bring you as much comfort in praying them as I found in writing them.

Part One

Expressing the Hurt

The Challenge of Honesty

There's no getting around it; this is a horrible time in your life, perhaps your worst time ever. Everything is darkness. Your trust in life's goodness has been replaced by rage at life's unfairness. Overwhelmed by sorrow, you cry at the slightest provocation. You can barely eat or sleep, let alone concentrate. Exhaustion intrudes. You wonder, Am I falling apart? Losing my mind? You're not just afraid; you're terrorized. A sense of desperation sets in. You feel utterly lost and alone. Surviving this time may be the hardest thing you'll ever do. What you're experiencing is a normal part of grief.

Survival requires emotional honesty. Give yourself permission to feel. Emotions aren't right or wrong; they just are. Denying them today causes problems tomorrow. Anger, guilt, fear, sadness, envy, loneliness, shock, and remorse—these are but a few of the feelings you may have. Prayer becomes particularly difficult because God seems absent. You feel forsaken. Thankfully, this feeling, while true on the emotional level, is false in reality, for God never leaves or forsakes us.

The faith that worked for you before will not sustain you now. Only when you realize that you have nothing left but God will you discover that God is enough. You must go deeper. If you're enraged at God for allowing your loss, then vent your rage as long and loudly as you need to. Do the same with all your emotions. If you're feeling weak and vulnerable, don't pretend to be strong. Rise to the challenge of emotional honesty, and you will find God in a new way. You will also participate in your own healing by grieving your loss through to resolution.

Faith Encounters Loss

Lord, I'm grieving. It hurts so bad.
My emotions are churning; my mind is racing;
my spirit is adrift.
I reach out to you because I have nowhere else to go.
> What I have lost I cannot regain—ever.
> It feels as if my life were over.
> How can I rebuild?
Chaos assaults me on all sides.
I see only darkness within and without.
> The pain, the uncertainty, the fear, the numbness—
> how will I ever get beyond these terrors?
You ask me to believe in you—
the God of perfect love—and I do.
> But why have you allowed this to happen?
> What good can come from such suffering?
I have no answers.
I have only you and your promise
never to leave or forsake me.
> May this be enough to get me through another day.
> I rest in you, my strength and my redeemer.
Please, oh please, stay by my side.
Cast me not away from your presence! Amen.

Absent God

Are you there, God?
I'm crying out to you, but I hear no response,
no whisper that you care,
no hint that you even exist.
   The old signposts are gone, the old certainties, lost.
   You seem so far from me now.
I never thought that life could wound me this way.
As I grieve, I feel so small, so alone.
   The past seems like a dream;
   the present, a nightmare;
   the future, an unbearable burden.
The ground has shifted beneath me;
I have no place to stand.
   I feel desperate, unable to function, unable to cope.
Am I losing my mind?
Or is this horror an opportunity
to learn the real meaning of faith?
   Be my rock, I pray.
O God of miracles,
give me the resources I need to survive.
   Help me to believe that I will feel better soon,
   that life after loss is worth living.
I do not ask to be rescued,
only to be restored to sanity.
   Bring this restoration soon, Lord.
   I need it today! Amen.

Enraged!

It's so unfair, God!
Why has life taken from me
what I fear I cannot live without?
   This cruelty has caught me off guard, and I'm angry!
   I never expected anything this devastating to happen to me.
I feel crushed. Why, I ask? Why me?
It seems futile to protest; protesting changes nothing.
   But what else can I do?
   Silence only intensifies my anguish and rage.
   At least I can tell you how I feel.
   Expressing a feeling helps to understand it,
   to grow beyond it.
I need to vent my indignation at this injustice.
True, I often took what I had for granted.
I seldom paused to give thanks, to savor my blessings.
   But from having to losing came so quickly.
   Does my lack of gratitude justify
   such a merciless reversal of fortune?
I'm trying to live the questions, Lord.
But each day is a struggle, tormented as I am
by visions of what was, but is no more.
   Help me to express my anger at you and life,
   at others and myself without turning it inward.
   May I accept life's unfairness
   without becoming bitter, O God.
In looking back with belated but sincere thanks,
and in looking ahead with faith,
I seek to be reconciled to my fate. Amen.

A Mountain in the Way

O you who are closer to me than my breath,
and more vital to me than my heartbeat,
I cry to you in my hour of need.
Hear my voice from within the dark tunnel of grief, I pray.
    I'm here not because I want to be
    but because I encountered a mountain on my journey—
    the mountain of loss.
The tunnel of grief leads to the other side of the mountain;
it's the only way through. I wish that it were different,
that I could go around or, better yet,
head in the other direction and return home.
    But you have other plans, O God.
    I must experience the desolation of this tunnel
    in order to discover my higher destiny.
Let me not be alarmed by my urge
to scream and shout, to run and hide.
May I recognize this urge as normal.
    Of course I'm feeling lost and overwhelmed, Lord.
    No other tunnel has prepared me for this one,
    and no other traveler can go through it for me.
Assure me that these turbulent emotions won't harm me.
Protect me from letting them cloud my judgment,
that I might not think or act in ways that I will later regret.
May I not repress these emotions, giving them power
over me, but find safe outlets for them,
that they won't haunt me forever.
    Take me over this mountain in your time,
    and I will build an altar
    in my heart to honor your faithfulness. Amen.

Terror at 3 A.M.

It's the middle of the night, dear Lord.
Again, I can't sleep.
   Questions besiege my mind,
   exploding my inner equilibrium.
   Fear and dread rampage within me
   like demons on the loose.
My hands shake. A knot grips my stomach.
A cold sweat forms on my brow.
   The terror time is here!
To survive this time will require
all of my strength and courage.
I have had challenges before, but never anything like this.
   My world has crumbled.
   I'm buried in the ruins and must find a way out, alone.
Stay with me until the morning, O God.
Be my companion and friend.
Watch and wait with me in my grief.
   Then I will arise from the ruins and discover
   the new world that awaits me beyond brokenness.
I can't do it without you, Lord.
I need you like I have never needed you before.
   Here we are, you and me alone in the night.
   Stay with me until dawn.
As the light comes,
so may your presence enlighten my heart. Amen.

Surrendering to the Process

O you who know my needs before I speak them
and my feelings before I express them,
thank you for the permission to grieve.
  I receive this permission as a gift in this moment.
  As I struggle to accept my loss and find healing,
  I need this gift more than any other.
Your permission to grieve reminds me
that it's okay to be lonely and sad, angry and afraid.
  Although I feel miserable right now, I can persevere,
  knowing that you don't condemn me for being human.
Free from condemnation,
I can surrender to the grief process,
learning its hard lessons on the way to rebirth.
  I'm silent before you, all-wise God,
  humbled by the finality of my loss,
  but emboldened by your compassion
  to be myself and to feel my emotions.
When I need to cry today, I will cry.
When I need to vent my anger, I will do it in a healthy way.
When I need support, I will call a friend.
  And I will not be ashamed!
Where this process will lead me I do not know.
  Go with me, O God, that it may lead
  toward heightened awareness
  and deepened character. Amen.

Letting the Tears Flow

Lord of the darkest midnight and the brightest dawn,
be with me as I cry.
   Assure me that it's okay to let it all out,
   to release every pent-up emotion.
My tears come from my deepest self.
I'm wounded there, cut and bleeding.
   The sad thoughts are flowing fast and furiously.
   They pummel me like tidal waves of pain.
I mourn what could have been, but now will never be.
Life was good to me for what seems
like a brief, golden moment.
Now the moment has passed, and I cry alone.
   Stay with me awhile, O Comforter of the brokenhearted.
   Enter into my sorrow as One who empathizes,
   as One who shares each sob and weeps
   each tear with me.
Give me the faith to believe that
"this, too, shall pass."
   But until it does, let me grieve freely and openly,
   knowing that there is no other way
   to protect my future happiness.
Accept me as I am, Lord—tears and all.
Then I can accept myself and rebuild my life,
confident that I am surrounded and upheld
by your mercy. Amen.

In Search of Shelter

Bear with me, good Lord, in my fragile condition.
How humiliated I feel to be so unstable.
    I'm not thinking clearly.
    My eating and sleeping patterns have been disrupted.
    A deep depression has settled into my soul.
Only my true friends try to understand.
Others dismiss me as self-absorbed,
a captive of a powerful inner upheaval.
    I feel self-conscious because I am not myself,
    and I can't hide it.
Being with happy people intensifies my loneliness.
Routine tasks trigger memories that break my heart.
A lump has lodged itself in my throat and won't go away.
    It's no use pretending.
    Grief's wound reveals itself in my forgetfulness,
    my nervousness, my moodiness.
This difficulty in coping staggers me, O God.
I come to you, my shelter in the time of storm,
as a wounded bird seeking a place of safety.
    Wrap me in your arms.
    Never let me go. Amen.

The Challenge
of Resiliency

There's only one phrase to describe your ordeal; it's what St. John of the Cross called "the dark night of the soul." In the dark night you feel dead and may wish you were dead. How does one get out of this place? It's a long journey characterized by two steps forward and three steps back. You must endure bad days and worse days to get to the better days. The good news is that the better days will come. In fact, if you do your grief work well, your best days are still ahead.

To reach these days, you must rise to the challenge of resiliency. To be resilient is to get up each time you're knocked down. It's to fight on, come what may. Doing this requires more strength than you have right now. Sufficient strength lies within you, but you can find and use it only with God's help. Take heart! God and the laws of nature are on your side. The psychologist C.G. Jung spoke of a flow toward wholeness at the center of life. Medical researchers call it the "the healing power of nature." As the body is designed to recover from disease, so the soul is equipped to heal from grief.

Prayer nurtures this healing. It invites God to suffer with us. Through prayer, ordinary people do the extraordinary. They raise handicapped children, live with debilitating health conditions, overcome addictions, and much more. They do this by relying on a Power beyond their own. This is the way of resiliency. As the German philosopher Nietzsche said, "Anything that doesn't kill me makes me stronger."

The Temptation to Quit

I'm fighting to keep my poise, O God.
It's almost impossible amid the burning flames of grief.
My instinct is to panic, to give up on myself and life.
A thousand voices within shout that my situation is hopeless,
that I will never smile or laugh again.

> Grieving tests my resolve; it reveals what I am made of.
> In this process I can increase my self-respect or diminish it.
> Will I quit, or fight on?
> By continuing to fight, I feel good about myself.

I don't want to be a quitter, Lord! But sometimes I am one.
This loss has created so many problems for me.
When they bear down on me, I crave an easy way out.

> Mighty and merciful God,
> reveal yourself to me in this struggle.
> Wean me from my lust for comfort and convenience.
> Create in me the determination to meet my challenges,
> come what may, and increase my resiliency
> as I refuse to be intimidated.

May I remember that I am running a marathon, not a sprint.
The miles get harder as the race wears on.
I am hot and sore, thirsty and tired.

> Quitting tempts me!

Only if you will run with me, O God, can I stay in the race.
Keep me moving toward the finish, Lord,
that I may wear the victor's wreath, having given my best.
Amen.

The Task at Hand

I'm trying to do the work of grief, O God.
And that's what it is—work.
>   Denying or avoiding my inner turmoil makes it worse.
>   The only way out is through.
I come to you, my unfailing Friend,
asking you to deliver me from the fantasy of a quick fix.
>   Grant me the wisdom to see that none exists.
May I not anesthetize my wounds
with alcohol, drugs, food, caffeine,
or other addictive substances or behaviors.
>   Rather, as I seek moderation in all things,
>   grant me access to a deeper inner strength
>   than I have ever known.
Teach me what it means
to be bruised but not beaten,
crushed but not defeated.
May I find in you a resiliency beyond my own,
and may I be sustained by the support
of a few compassionate soulmates.
>   Talking and weeping through my shock and numbness,
>   fear and guilt, anger and depression humbles me.
>   It also reminds me that when I am weak, then I am strong,
>   because only in my weakness do I learn to depend on you.
I am reaching out in the darkness, O God.
Grasp my hand in yours
and lead me through this perilous time.
>   Join me in the work of grief,
>   and I will labor on until I find your peace,
>   which passes understanding. Amen.

Coming Back

O God of great reversals, who brings day out of night,
spring out of winter, life out of death,
I seek a turning point as I strive to come back from my loss.
I have been foundering for too long.
I am like a ship in a storm
trying to find my way back to port.
  The howling wind, the driving rain,
  the crashing waves of sadness—
  they buffet my soul and threaten to sink me.
  Is it possible, O God, to be in the storm
  without letting the storm be in me?
I ask not for protection but for perseverance.
Making it to the safe harbor of recovery
means following you when I can't see where you're leading.
  May I keep following in spite of my doubts,
  that I may learn that doubt is not the opposite of faith,
  but an element within faith.
  Certainty is the opposite of faith.
Lead me on, precious Lord, when uncertainty
obscures the way ahead.
Help me to interpret setbacks not as defeats
but as nurturers of resiliency.
Aided by this interpretation,
I am continuing to come back from my loss.
  Go before me, O God, that the storm may be stilled
  and I may find rest in your embrace. Amen.

Suffering with God

How can my grief be redeemed, O God?
Can anything good come of it?
    I seek spiritual insight into this excruciating experience.
    Perhaps this is it: When I grieve, I am like you.
    Your heart breaks over every human sorrow,
    every triumph of evil, every choice of indifference and fear
    over involvement and faith.
I share your hurt, O God.
I, too, have a broken heart.
Things didn't go my way this time.
A treasured part of my life is gone for good.
    It was inevitable,
    for no relationship or experience lasts forever.
    May I retain my self-worth by not
    becoming withdrawn and reclusive.
    Such a cynical response only makes matters worse.
Instead, show me new ways to keep involved in life
and to reach out to others.
    This is what you do.
    You never give up.
    You keep loving no matter the risk.
Thank you for setting this example.
Help me to follow it in every endeavor,
trusting that it's better to love and lose
than never to love at all. Amen.

The Rewards of Patience

Help me to accept that I am where I need to be
in the grief process, O God.
>   Sometimes its challenges overwhelm me,
>   especially when recycling through its stages
>   or getting hit by all stages at once.
When this happens, I am plunged into turmoil,
convinced that I can't go on.
>   But I must.
>   For reasons I don't understand,
>   you allow this process to take
>   more than a day, a week, or a month.
I may be walking this road for several years,
and some parts of it must be traveled
more than once.
>   O God of the wide earth and open sky,
>   grant me safe passage.
>   Teach me something valuable at every turn.
Hold the goal of transfigured life before me always,
but let me not condemn myself for being slow to reach it.
Rather, make me as patient with my humanness as you are.
>   If you let me be where I am without judging me,
>   should I not do likewise?
>   Whether I am advancing, retreating,
>   or holding my ground,
>   grant me the assurance that I am moving ahead spiritually.
I sense this movement when the quietness within me
triumphs over the clamor. Let me nurture this quietness
here and now, that all may be well with my soul. Amen.

Keeping Your Perspective

The child in me expects life to be fair, O God.
It seems only right that good people
should be protected from tragedy,
that only bad people should suffer.
   But often the opposite happens.
   The wrong people prosper,
   and the wrong people get hurt.
When victimized by unfairness,
I throw inner tantrums of rage.
I lose my center in your love and see life not as
a gift from your hand but as a chamber of horrors.
   I need a new perspective,
   a more mature way of looking at things.
   Once I stop expecting fairness,
   I can appreciate life for what it is,
   not for what I wish it were.
When realism tempers my naivete,
I make wiser choices and become
less vulnerable to disappointment.
   Put to death the childishness within me, O Lord.
   Help me to accept life on its own terms,
   realizing that its potential for suffering
   enriches its joys.
When tragedy strikes, remind me that
you still have the last word.
Increase my resiliency in the face of unfairness.
As you care for the birds of the air
and the flowers of the field,
so do I ask you to care for me. Amen.

The Hero's Response

Dear God, I keep thinking that my life has been ruined.
So many of my hopes have been dashed.
When I look out at the future,
all I see are dead ends and "no exit" signs.
Suffering loss seems to have condemned me
to a meaningless existence.

> Remind me that you are the God of
> restored hopes and new beginnings.
> With you, there is no such thing as a ruined life.
> You call me to adventure in good times and bad.
> Let me respond affirmatively by accepting
> the challenge of the hero's journey.

I must do battle with despair and emerge victorious.
Deliver me from negativity and defeatism.
Help me to believe in miracles.
May I remember that every crisis contains
the seeds of both peril and promise.

> You want me to respond with hope,
> with an attitude that never stops believing
> in a better life. I can only do this
> as I draw on the resiliency that
> you placed within me at my making.

Thank you for the flow toward wholeness at the center of life.
Because of this healing stream,
I need not be intimidated by my new circumstances.
The resources needed to deal with them are within me.
Accompany me on the adventure of finding these resources,
and the hero's journey will guide me to a better future. Amen.

Part Two

Seeking
the
Healing

The Challenge of Receptivity

Some gifts come only when you are grieving. Allowed to choose, you would rather not receive them; you would prefer to have back what you lost. But you weren't allowed to choose. Thus the challenge of receptivity confronts you. You meet this challenge by opening your heart to grace. This will take time, but open your heart you must. Your healing depends on it.

Grace is the greatest gift of grief. An indestructible goodness at life's center, grace is God having the last word. Grace is any sign of triumph coming from tragedy, any gift that you freely receive but don't deserve. Grace is God meeting you at the point of your need. When grief strands you in a spiritual wilderness, you may lose faith in grace. But regaining that faith offers the only way out. The sun rises and sets each day. The seasons come and go. You have food, clothing, shelter, and people who love you. That's grace.

Grace can't be manipulated; it breaks through in surprising ways. Nor is grace magic, but it works true miracles in the heart. How do you experience grace? By surrendering to life's mystery and embracing despair as well as hope. You can't go back and be the person you were before your loss; you can only move ahead, sadder but wiser. Many gifts await you beyond grief: greater compassion, truer humility, freer acceptance, deeper courage, and gratitude. Each is a gift of grace. Be receptive to them as you pray, and your prayers will be answered in your own spiritual growth.

A Welcome for an Unwelcome Guest

O God of all goodness and every blessing,
help me to bring an open heart to my grief.
    Thus far I have not done so.
    Grief came unexpectedly to me,
    an uninvited guest knocking at my door.
I wanted to send the guest away.
Help me to be more welcoming, Lord.
    Perhaps this guest has something special to give me—
    a lesson in receiving grace.
I learn this lesson when I live my life
inwardly in communion with my depths,
upwardly in relationship with your Spirit,
and outwardly in concern for others.
    As I hear your call to receptivity,
    may I grow in compassion and courage.
    Only by grace will I grow in these ways and
    not let my grief destroy me.
Teach me to focus more on the goodness at life's center
than on the evil and tragedy at its fringes.
Fortify my confidence that goodness
will eventually triumph
and put an end to crying and pain.
    May that end come for me as my grief forces me
    to rely on your grace as my hope of salvation.
    Then I will extend a welcome to this unwelcome guest
    and be freed to heal at last. Amen.

To Worry No More

Calm me down, Lord; calm me down.
When worry intrudes into my mind,
threatening to overwhelm me,
bring me back to my center in you.
  My loss has changed my life so much.
  Everything is different now.
I need the assurance that all things work together
for good in order to survive this time.
This assurance is grace, through which I find
the pardon, power, and promise to redeem my life.
  May your grace be as a candle burning within me,
  a reminder that I am part of your good creation
  in spite of my shortcomings and sins.
May your grace be as the sun shining above me,
a witness to life's ongoing rhythm
that will eventually heal all wounds.
  May your grace be as a pillar of fire
  illuminating the way before me,
  an invitation to take heart as I step
  into the unknown.
Calm me down, Lord; calm me down.
Shine the light of your grace
not only within, above, and before me,
but also behind, below, and beside me.
  Surrounded by your presence,
  I worry no more, for I know that
  I am safe in the hollow of your hand.
  For this, and for all good things, I give thanks. Amen.

On Eagle's Wings

To whom can I turn but to you, unchanging God,
when I need stability for my life?
    Never have I needed it more
    than in the aftermath of my loss.
I seek the stability that comes
not from my own efforts
but from sharing in your wholeness.
Teach me that stability can't be earned;
it's a gift of grace.
    When will I stop seeking this gift in external things?
    I have been doing this for so long
    that it's hard to change, Lord.
But I now have no alternative but to change.
My loss has confronted me with the folly
of my spiritual immaturity.
    This time, I am forced to look within to find
    the truth that undergirds my life and tells me who I am.
    Make this a sacred moment by empowering me to claim
my personhood apart from anyone else's approval.
Encounter me with your presence in my inner being,
and I will discover the only source of lasting stability,
which is your grace within me.
    May this encounter teach me that suffering
    is not meaningless, but a catalyst of creativity
    when endured in faith.
As I seek this endurance, may I renew my strength;
may I mount up on wings as eagles;
may I run and not grow weary
walk and not faint. Amen.

Goodbye to Guilt

They say that hindsight is twenty/twenty, O Lord.
If I could live my life over,
I would do so many things differently.
   Oh, for a second chance!
There are words I would have spoken,
promises I would have kept,
sacrifices I would have made,
love I would have shared.
   But it's too late now.
   Yesterday is gone, its relationships and
   experiences irretrievable except as memories.
Guilt stalks me in unguarded moments.
Help me to say goodbye to it, O God,
and to the self-condemnation it inspires.
   Rather than look back with regret,
   may I look ahead with expectation.
Remind me that, because of your grace,
mistakes can be redeemed,
wounds can be healed,
relationships can be restored or released.
   It's time to let go of everything
   I can't change and get on with my life.
I give the past to you, O God.
Grant me the wisdom to acknowledge my failures,
the willingness to receive your forgiveness,
and the faith to believe in a new tomorrow. Amen.

Believing without Understanding

Lord of love and Lord of life,
I don't always understand your ways
or events that happen in your world,
but I know I need you.
    Not as a crutch do I need you,
        but as a guiding presence that attends my way.
My loss has confronted me with the dark side of life.
Tragedies strike. Relationships end. People die.
I am trying to accept that you allow bad things
to happen but are still good, O God.
    This is my ongoing challenge.
    Increase my faith, that I may continue believing
        in your power and love, though you allow suffering.
Remind me that I wouldn't want to live
in a random universe. Without laws of nature
that apply to all, chaos would reign.
I ask you not to prevent nature from hurting me,
but to guard me against hurting myself with bad choices.
    O God, who creates everyone equal
        in vulnerability, may I love you for
        the ways you allow yourself to be vulnerable, too.
May I worship you without having to understand you
and celebrate my blessings while I can,
for tomorrow my fortunes may change.
Grant me your grace amid these changes,
and I will serve you forever. Amen.

Comfort from the Past

God of every time and place,
grief sends memories rippling through my mind
like the windblown water of a mountain lake.
   The good times and the bad times
   are part of my inner world,
   part of the spiritual experience
   that makes me who I am.
My memories can make my heart tender;
they can also bring it encouragement.
May I receive every good memory as a gift of your grace.
   I close my eyes and see faces now gone,
   streets and homes now changed,
   images of myself now transformed from youth to maturity.
Thank you that I have much to treasure from the past.
Although my loss has devastated me,
I won't let it take everything.
   The special moments I have known
   still burn brightly in my spirit. I reclaim them now.
Thank you for the wonders of my childhood—
the grass beneath my feet, the adventures with friends,
the discoveries made in school.
   Let me not forget the successes I enjoyed
   in growing up, which infused my spirit
   with a sense of inner approval.
Most of all, bring to my mind the relationships
that have sustained me across the years.
May I find new people with whom to share my life now,
that memories of today will comfort me in the future
as I am comforted today by memories of the past. Amen.

Song of Courage

From the dissonant sound of fear within me,
I turn to you, O God of perfect harmony.
   I have not felt like singing in a long time.
   How I wish I did!
I remember when music filled my days,
sending me on my way inspired,
ready to meet any challenge.
   I long to hear the music again.
O Lord who makes trembling hearts brave,
attune the ears of my spirit
to your eternal refrains of courage.
   Renew my trust that those refrains never end,
   that they play on
   in spite of grief's efforts to silence them.
May I listen now.
   So many fears assail me.
   I lie awake at night worrying
   about my finances, my family, my future.
I have fears about my health, my job, my relationships.
Sometimes I feel that my fears are driving me insane!
   Let me not believe that I can be brave on my own.
   Remind me that courage is a gift of your grace,
   that I can't manufacture it, only surrender to it.
Turn my mourning into dancing as I hear
your song of courage and learn to sing it myself.
This is the melody that helps to mend a broken heart.
Do your work of mending now, O God,
and my lips will sound forth your praise. Amen.

The Challenge of Creativity

The word "creative" has a hopeful sound. To create is to bring something new into being, something never before known. A healthy grief process invites you to join God in doing this. Your loss shattered your inner world; you can't rebuild it the way it was. Creativity is needed to fashion something beautiful out of the brokenness. Your identity must be reconfigured, but that can't happen unless you draw on inner resources you have yet to tap. Only then will you see possibilities, not just problems, in your situation. Such maturity of vision is a sign of a creative response. By grieving your loss through to resolution, you emerge a new person. From crisis can come character. Such is the promise of transformation.

Your loss has brought your inner issues to the surface. You can work on them and grow—or deny them and stagnate. Perhaps some soul-searching is in order. How do you see yourself? Where do you need to change? What's really important to you? What relationships are calling for your attention? Would you benefit from spiritual direction or psychotherapy?

This is the discipline of living the questions. Often there are no answers. The questions themselves go deeper than words. Sitting with them in prayer, you can eventually respond to them creatively and find inner renewal. Thus you end up in a different place on the other side of grief. But transformation happens slowly. You can't rush it. Surrendering your loss to God, you finally let it go; you accept it. Practicing this acceptance enables you to live not as a victim but as a survivor, and eventually, a wounded healer. Life has changed, but life goes on. It's up to you to make the best of it.

More than Second Best

I come to you, O God of resurrection and renewal,
to reorient my thinking.
   I have been idealizing the life I knew before my loss.
   From the perspective of today,
   yesterday looks so perfect,
   a fantasy of fulfillment and abundance.
Then came the devastation that changed everything.
   Now my possibilities seem so limited,
   so mundane compared with what could have been.
Silence in me this worn-out lament
about how incomparable life used to be.
Speak to me instead about the growth and learning,
friendship and accomplishment, beauty and joy
that await me in times to come.
   Inspire in me a creative response to life after loss,
   that you and I together may fashion
   a masterpiece from the ashes.
Guard me from seeing this life as second-best,
as if you offer only one chance at happiness,
and to miss it is never to regain it.
   Anoint my soul with the oil of hope, dear Lord.
   Then I will believe that the best is yet to be,
   that I have only begun to discover the surprises
   you have in store for me.
Open my heart to these surprises, O God,
that the resurrection life you want for me
will be mine at last. Amen.

Discovery in the Wasteland

Shepherd of love, you risk everything to seek and find me,
even leaving the flock to do so.
    My mind affirms this;
    my heart wants to affirm it also,
    but it can't until I move
    from self-pity to self-giving,
    from melting down to beginning again.
This wasteland through which I have been wandering
has disoriented and confused me.
I feel alienated from you and others and myself.
    Take me beyond the pain, Lord.
    You are the Good Shepherd
    who makes me lie down in green pastures,
    who leads me beside still waters,
    who restores my soul.
Show me how I need to change
to reach this place of restoration and refreshment.
Let me surrender to the creative process
that surviving grief requires.
Deny to me any illusions about this process being easy.
    Grant me the faith to follow you
    for the long haul, Lord.
    Not someone else's faith do I need,
    but my own, a faith that forges
    redemption from the suffering of my life.
Whatever inner work is required to attain this faith,
let me do it now, that the wasteland may be for me
not a place of defeat but a place of discovery. Amen.

Dreams that Heal

God of every yesterday and every tomorrow,
grant me a vision of things to come.
May it be a vision of life being good again.
    It seems like a dream that
    the old enthusiasm could return to my spirit,
    the old bounce to my step,
    the old smile to my lips.
But I must dream in order to hope.
    Here in the silence I close my eyes
    and see myself happy again.
    The tears have all been dried,
    the fears silenced,
    the nerves calmed.
I see myself welcoming each new day as an adventure.
I am eating and sleeping well,
enjoying the company of friends,
setting new goals, feeling good about life.
I have rejoined the human race!
    Today this dream seems impossible to achieve.
    It's higher than my reach, wider than my embrace.
I need your help, O God.
Reveal your creativity within me,
that I may be transformed by your love.
Then I will dream again,
and all will be well with my heart. Amen.

Claiming Your Uniqueness

Out of my distortions and into your truth,
out of my evasions and into your honesty,
out of my perplexity and into your peace,
I come, O God, to you.

Confront me with my real self
and my real situation, I pray.
Help me to keep my pain in perspective.
Catastrophizing makes it worse.
May I be thankful for what has not been taken from me.

Whatever my limitations physically or emotionally,
I still have the opportunity to grow,
to nurture the uniqueness
that you planted in me at my making.

I am trusting that this loss has a purpose
in your design for my life. As I struggle
to make sense of it, may I become a new person,
intimately connected to my depths,
awakened in consciousness.

Having integrated my loss into my identity,
may I be tempered and matured, not overwhelmed,
by life's adversities.

Then I will find my true self,
that special gift you have waiting
for me when I have endured enough
and learned enough to receive it.

My palms are open, Lord; let me
receive it today. Amen.

Transformation and Travail

One day at a time, Lord.
That's what I need to remember.
The radical restructuring taking place
within me will not happen overnight.
    But I forget this.
    I want to feel terrific now. This minute!
To be able to order my pain away,
talk it away, medicate it away—
this seems like the perfect solution,
an easy escape from grief's travail.
    But without travail there can be no transformation.
    Birth pangs accompany each birth.
    They are the price I must pay
    to be born anew in wholeness.
I claim this wholeness now.
You are the God who makes all things new,
who brings forth spring from winter,
dawn from darkness, life from death.
    Use your creative power
    to bring forth wholeness in me, O God.
    I surrender to your power in this moment.
Fill me with your presence and
drive from my soul every negative emotion.
Surround me with your holy angels.
Grant me a vision of your glory.
Use my travail to make me a more spiritual person.
    One day at a time, Lord.
    Keep me moving toward transformation in you,
    one day at a time. Amen.

Impossible Possibilities

O God of redeemed yesterdays and bright tomorrows,
I need a miracle.
Nothing less will do in this situation.
You have done it before, Lord.
When I look back and see your hand of blessing upon me,
I give thanks.
 You have always provided enough work to keep me busy,
 enough health to keep me strong,
 enough love from others to keep me sane.
Perform one more miracle in my life, I pray.
I ask not that you would change my circumstances
but that you would change me.
Awaken my heart and fill it with new life.
Instead of fear, grant me faith; instead of anger,
understanding; instead of guilt and depression,
grace and peace.
 Allow me a glimpse of tomorrow.
 May it be a glimpse of life at its best.
Only you can take me beyond what is to what can be.
As you helped me to survive a terrifying crisis,
so may I help others who find themselves
in the dark night of the soul.
 Sunsets and waterfalls and rainbows
 are miracles of your creation, O God.
 Make me a miracle, too, as I share
 with the world the compassion and hope
 you have shared with me. Amen.

Remembering the Goal

O God for whom all things are possible,
dig the well of acceptance deep within me.
I need to draw from this well whenever
I encounter something I cannot change.

But my well of acceptance often runs dry, Lord.
One moment I am living creatively,
my loss behind me, my grief resolved.
The next moment I am back to square one—
numb or sad, angry or guilty, afraid or depressed again.

Giver of all good gifts, I want it to be different today.
Enough of this futile cycle!
I am tired of drinking deeply of acceptance one day
and going thirsty the next.

Teach me, Lord, that this is part of the process
from which my transformed self will evolve.
No one's well of acceptance is fathomless.
The well deepens over time,
its waters increasing in value with age,
like fine wine.
May I seek this wine always, remembering that
its attainment is worth any sacrifice.

Oh, to live in acceptance! To stop lamenting
life's cruelties, to make peace with everything
I cannot change—how energizing this would be.
I seek this energy by offering my whole self to you, O God.
Here are my wounds and needs, my interests and abilities,
my relationships and dreams. Help me to take the good
along with the bad, as you have,
and live in your freedom. Amen.

The Daybreak Within

O God of the eternal sunrise and the invincible springtime,
I greet the daybreak in my soul today.
Your creative work has triumphed.
    Just for today I will believe in the dawn.
    I will walk not in the shadows of death
    but in the morning of rebirth.
Life has moved on; so have I.
I am not the person I was before my loss.
Having survived this trauma, I am more confident now,
better prepared to fight any battle.
    Just for today I will not concentrate on the hurt,
    but celebrate the healing in my life.
The healing has not come all at once, O God.
But it's on its way; I can feel it.
May the certainty of recovery be my strength.
I don't want any more sojourns
in the land of despair.
    Rivet my attention to the sunrise, Lord.
    Every morning it comes. Nothing can hold it back,
    not cloudy skies or hurricane winds,
    not raging seas or deafening thunderclaps. Nothing!
So may your healing come in my heart,
radiant and righteous God.
Just for today, lift my eyes higher than my problems,
and fill me with the wonder of your creation.
Unleash your transforming power in me,
and the person I become, like the sunrise,
will belong fully to you. Amen.

Of Related Interest...

They Shall Be Comforted
For Those Who Grieve and Hope—Reflections, Readings, Prayers, Rituals
Rev. Joseph Nolan

This useful resource is for the dying, their loved ones and those who minister to them. It will be appreciated by pastoral ministers and families for wakes and funeral services.

0-89622-978-5, 144 pp, $9.95 (J-23)

Surviving Death
A Practical Guide to Caring for the Dying & Bereaved
Charles Meyer

A helpful and inspirational handbook for all who deal with and care for the dying and their surviving families. The experience and insights of a hospital chaplain are here for all of us.

0-89622-486-4, 200 pp, $9.95 (W-76)

Praying with the Sick
Prayers, Services, Rituals
Sandra DeGidio, OSM

A valuable handbook and resource for anyone who ministers to the sick. The author offers practical suggestions with an empathetic approach, and the prayers cover a broad spectrum of needs.

0-89622-893-2, 64 pp, $6.95 (B-88)

A Thoughtful Word, A Healing Touch
A Guide for Visiting the Sick
Joseph M. Champlin & Susan Champlin Taylor

Filled with helpful hints and wise guidance for making bedside visits an occasion of hope and consolation. Includes Scripture readings and prayers for healing.

0-89622-637-9, 40 pp, $2.95 (M-19)

Available at religious bookstores or from:

TWENTY-THIRD PUBLICATIONS
A Division of Bayard PO BOX 180 • MYSTIC, CT 06355
1-800-321-0411 • FAX: 1-800-572-0788 • E-MAIL: ttpubs@aol.com
www.twentythirdpublications.com

Call for a free catalog